The Forgotten Man of Christmas

Joseph's Story

Howard Edington

Foreword by Dr. Bill Bright

Synchronicity
press

Published by InSync Communications LLC and Synchronicity Press
2445 River Tree Circle
Sanford, FL 32771
http://www.insynchronicity.com

Library of Congress Catalog Number: 00-103408
          Edington, Howard, 1942 -
The Forgotten Man of Christmas: Joseph's Story
          ISBN: 1-929902-01-8

Second Synchronicity Press Printing
10 9 8 7 6 5 4 3 2

Synchronicity Press books are available at special discounts when purchased in bulk for use in seminars, as premiums, or in sales promotions. Special editions or book excerpts can also be created to specification, For details, contact InSync Communications LLC at the address above.

Cover Design by Jonathan Pennell
Book Design & Composition by Stephanie Murphy

Printed in the United States of America

For our son
John David Edington
October 8, 1972 – December 21, 1994
"A young man forever in the Kingdom of Heaven"

Table of Contents

Acknowledgments

My thanks to the following:

- Trisha Edington, my partner in life and love, who urged me to write this book as a way of remembering our son John David on the fifth anniversary of his death, and who then patiently took my words and fashioned them into written pages.
- David Dodson, my brother-in-law, whose sharp eye for the language proved invaluable in clarifying my own thoughts.
- Dennis McClellan, who believed enough in me and in this project to be willing to publish it.
- Bill Bright, who in spite of a world-encircling ministry through Campus Crusade, has taken the time to become a faithful member of my church, a true friend, and a partner in prayer.
- Bill Peterson, Rob Bullock, and Pam Theall, members of my church's staff, who provided faithful and capable technical support along the way.
- Bryan Harden, dynamic Director of Music and the Arts at First Presbyterian in Orlando, who first introduced me to the song "Joseph's Lullaby," the words of which stretched my own understanding of the man known as the Carpenter of Nazareth.
- Anne and Bill Robbinson, whose Kenmure home in the mountains gave us time to pray hard and study deeply.
- Bettie and Joseph Whitaker, who graciously permitted Trisha and me to sequester ourselves amidst the splendors of their lakeside estate in order to complete the writing of these pages.
- My children and grandchildren – Meg, Bill, and Penn Sefton and Beth, Bobby, and Hunter Hewitt – who have given me the joy of loving them and who have loved me in return, making my own experience as a father not unlike that of Joseph's.

Foreword

by
Dr. Bill Bright
Campus Crusade for Christ

What if you lived in a society with a strict moral code and were engaged to a young girl who, during the engagement period, was discovered to be pregnant by someone other than yourself?

Then while you were contemplating breaking the engagement, what if an angel appeared to you in a dream one night and told you that God Himself had made her pregnant, and that she would give birth to One who would be the Saviour promised by more than 300 prophecies hundreds of years before? This would make you the human step-father of God in the flesh!

This once-in- history experience happened to a man named Joseph, a unique and privileged man for all the ages, described so eloquently by my pastor, Dr. Howard Edington.

Dr. Edington is one of the most effective communicators of the Good News of Jesus Christ in our time. His messages are always based upon Scripture and designed to exalt our Lord. He often begins his sermons with prayers such as, "Nothing in my hand I bring, simply to Thy cross I cling." Or, "Give me Jesus; you can have all the rest, just give me Jesus." I find myself sitting on the edge of my seat in anticipation of his creative content and heartwarming illustrations.

As you read this inspiring book, *The Forgotten Man of Christmas*, you too will be on the edge of your seat. You will not want to put it down until you finish this adventure with Howard, who with great skill describes Joseph's vitally important role in God's great drama of history, such as his gracious loving care of the Virgin Mary – obeying God's command given to him by the angel and trusting all that God said about her to be true.

We have biblical reasons to believe that Joseph was an excellent model and mentor to our Lord Jesus from His cradle until His ascension to be with the Father.

Joseph was indeed one of the most important figures in all history. This is because of his godly life and influence in the life of the greatest woman who ever lived, the Virgin Mary, and in the life of her Son, our Lord Jesus Christ, the Son of God, the promised Messiah, the greatest Person who ever lived.

As you read, be prepared to meet not only Joseph, but also his adopted son, Jesus, who is in the life-changing business. No doubt you will want to love and follow Him with Howard, myself, and hundreds of millions of others all over the world, in every nation. When you meet Him, you will never be the same. When you come to know Him, you will experience His love, joy and peace for ever and ever, life without end.

Prologue

I am thrilled by Easter.

It sets my spirit to soaring and my lips to singing as it trumpets the resurrection hope of victory over death and evil.

I am moved by Pentecost.

It drives me to my knees in thanks for God's gift to us of both His Spirit and His Church for the transformation of individual lives and the societies of which we are a part.

But I *love* Christmas.

I love its joy and caring, its expectancy and excitement. I love its bright lights, glowing candles, red flowers, smiling faces. I love its childish squeals, its embracing love, its lilting music. I love its stories… of shepherds on hillsides hearing symphonies of angels, of the Son of God being lulled to sleep in an animal feed box, of mysterious Easterners traveling great distances bearing exquisite gifts. I love the veil of holy hush Christmas drapes over the cacophony of a hurly-burly world, if only for a scant twenty-four hours. I love the best wishes, the best intentions, the best thoughts, the best motivations Christmas calls forth, if only fleetingly, from Christian and non-Christian alike. I love the promise of peace that Christmas dangles so tantalizingly. I love Christmas.

The most vivid childhood memories carry me back to Christmas Day celebrations in my grandparents' home in Mobile, Alabama, where five nuclear families would gather around an immense dining room table in a palpable explosion of love and joy.

Ground Zero of Christmas celebrations was my grandmother, "Mamán." The undisputed matriarch of the family, Mamán believed that Christmas existed for one purpose and one purpose only: to celebrate the birth of her Saviour. This simple insight required that Christmas at her house be celebrated with great flourish. One of the most memorable celebrations deserves special mention. As we gathered at a table that groaned beneath the weight of a great Christmas feast, Mamán stood at the head of the table and decreed that we should now all stand, light sparklers, hold them high and sing "Joy to the World." The pyrotechnic effect was far more spectacular than she ever imagined! The sparklers, when lighted, began plopping molten balls of flame right onto the dining room table, igniting the nylon table decorations on contact. Those of my generation who witnessed the conflagration will forever carry the indelible image of our horrified parents, risking life and limb to snuff the flames with their napkins while Mamán stood at the head of the table, sparkler held heavenward, eyes closed in dignified emotion and devotion. With beatitude welling from her sainted face, Mamán made a joyful noise at the top of her glorious voice, blissfully unaware of the total chaos around her. What a Christmas!

Today in my own home, the Thanksgiving dishes are hardly dry before we spangle our home with the signs of the Christmas season. These constant reminders remain in full and vigorous control of our decor until the "Twelfth Day of Christmas." It's one of those customs every family uses to give life for as long as possible to the wondrous lift of the season.

And while I always enjoy exercising the preaching gift which is mine from God, I must tell you that preaching during the Christmas season is downright fun.

I *love* Christmas!

Perhaps it is because I am a man of simple faith that Christmas holds such appeal for me. Christmas reduces the intricate theological complexity of Christianity to basic elements of truth even a child — or the most childlike among us — can accept and understand. The stories of Christmas – deeply entwined in the fabric of our cultural literacy — are marvelous tapestries of truth and legend, woven throughout the centuries and carefully hung in the halls of our collective memory. The chronicles delight and, in some cases, disturb — but they are evergreen —

always current and perennially popular, passed faithfully and joyously from generation to generation.

The biblical accounts of the First Christmas are limited to the first two chapters of the Gospels of Matthew and Luke. The material contained in those four chapters runs deep in our consciousness. When you hear, "In those days a decree went out from Caesar Augustus..." a team of horses could not stop your mind from forming the words, "...that all the world should be taxed..." Despite this awesome power of the unadorned Scriptural accounts, we have embroidered the Scriptural story of Christmas with the glittery stuff of legend from time to time.

A case in point is Matthew 2:1 where we are told that "...Magi from the East came to Jerusalem..." That is the sum total of Matthew's account of these mysterious men from the East and their mission. However, the tradition of the Church has nailed down details never revealed in the Bible. For instance, we have pinpointed the number of Magi (Wise Men) at three, which matches well with the gifts of gold, frankincense, and myrrh. We have bestowed the title "king" on the three visitors and attired them in royal robes. We routinely depict them astride camels, though no such designation is found in the Bible. Tradition has assigned them three different ethnic backgrounds, even given the men names — Caspar, Melchior, and Balthasar.

Some folks are concerned that mixing such legendary details with the Biblical truth somehow renders the Gospel account invalid, making a mockery of our celebration of Christmas. I don't think they should worry too much. To enjoy Parson Weems' musings about George Washington's unfortunate encounter with a cherry tree in no way undermines the validity of our Republic or the integrity of spirit upon which this nation was founded. Quite the contrary: Such positive legends serve to make the truth even more available to our minds.

Precisely the same thing occurs in many Christmas stories. If it is simply legend that the Wise Men represented the three major ethnic strains, what a wonderful legend it is, for it serves as a clever reminder that Jesus Christ destroys the racial barriers separating people from each other. We are "all made one in Christ." To have that great Biblical truth from Galatians reinforced for us every Christmas in the traditional story of the Wise Men is one more blessing of the season.

Other people worry that since the Christmas stories, particularly the Virgin Birth, are mentioned in a few verses of Matthew and Luke and nowhere else, the stories must have been appended to Scripture by the later tradition of the Church and therefore do not reflect historical reality. I do not buy that for a moment! I have been much enlightened on this point by the work of Scotland's James Orr. He contends, rightly I think, that Matthew records Joseph's personal eyewitness account of the First Christmas, while Luke provides us with the same story from Mary's point of view.

Read the two accounts carefully. You will realize that they are filled with such personal events, insights, and thoughts (dreams, visitations from angels, Mary's song, *etc*.) that the only way we could have known of these things is for Mary and Joseph themselves to have told them. How much more substantial can you get?

Understood in that light and taken together, the two accounts provided the Early Church with the full and complete story. Not only that, but given the unimpeachable source of the material — Mary and Joseph — the Early Church saw no need to further amplify, explain, or interpret the accounts found in Matthew or Luke. They stood then, and they stand now, on their own. They are nothing less than the personal testimony of Jesus' earthly parents.

As James Orr puts it, "I cannot see how these stories received the unchallenged reception of the Church unless it was understood and believed that such was their origin." I cling to the same belief. While tradition may have gilded the stories with some details, the Matthew and Luke accounts, plain and unvarnished, have about them the crystal clear ring of truth. I accept them as such.

My impression has been that in our time, we have tended to focus the attention of our worship, preaching, and study upon Mary's telling of the story in Luke. Because of Joseph's relegation to the role of bit player in the Christmas drama, we have tended to neglect his personal account as recorded in Matthew. Consequently, in an effort to provide a corrective for my own preaching and devotional life, I have immersed myself in a study of Matthew, chapters 1 and 2.

To my great surprise I discovered something I had missed previously. During the events surrounding the First Christmas, God spoke directly to Joseph in four separate dreams. Each of those dreams proved pivotal in the unfolding Christmas events, and Joseph's responses to the dreams are loaded with spiritual instructions applicable to our own journeys of faith. Reading Matthew with new eyes opened a significant and beautiful dimension to the Christmas story, and that experience led to the book you hold in your hands. It is my earnest hope and prayer that this little volume will add a new facet of understanding to your own celebration of Christmas and that it will help you to love Christmas as much as I do.

Howard Edington
Palazzo del Lago
Windermere, Florida
August, 1999

⮑ DREAM ONE ⮐

EMBARRASSMENT

He is, I think, the forgotten figure of the Christmas story. I refer to Joseph, the carpenter of Nazareth...

Our Christmas cards portray the Babe in Bethlehem, the mother and the manger, the herdsmen on the hillsides, the Wise Men and the angels—but where is Joseph? In the Christmas carols, we sing of "Virgin mother and child"... "Angels from the realms of glory"... "Shepherds in the fields abiding"... "We three kings of Orient are"... even "O little town of Bethlehem"— but what of Joseph?

He is the forgotten man of Christmas.

In the Word of God, Joseph stands silent. He is spoken to and he is spoken about, but not a single syllable crosses his lips. He is viewed at best as just a bit player, an extra, in the Christmas drama. Over the years, we have unconsciously, and I presume, unintentionally, ignored him and pushed him into the background.

However, to my way of thinking he deserves to be front and center together with Mary and the Child. For while he may not be acclaimed in our cards and carols, and while he may not spring to the forefront of our Christmas consciousness, nevertheless he is vitally important because of what God said to him and what God did through him. His faith, his courage, his strength, his sensitivity, his compassion, his devotion, his determination, his foresight, and his obedience to the will of God actually have a greater impact on Christian thought and on the Christian lifestyle than we have been willing to acknowledge.

Of course coming to a deeper understanding of Joseph is easier said than done because we do know so little about him. As a friend said to me in encouraging my work on this book,

1

"I'd like to see you give Joseph at least some clothes and an I.D." Here's a stab at it: As a descendant of King David and a scion of the wandering tribes of warrior herdsmen of Judea, Joseph's features no doubt would have been dark, his beard thick, his hair full and curly. Given the nature of his occupation, his clothing would have been simple, probably homespun, perhaps accentuated with bands of color, reminiscent of the Old Testament Joseph's "coat of many colors." Perhaps not. We cannot know for sure.

We can assume that he would have been a strong man physically, possessing the sturdy frame and taut sinews of one accustomed to long hours of hard work handling heavy weights. His hands would have been large and worn as befits a craftsman, yet his touch would have remained sensitive enough to feel the proper fit of an oxen's yoke or the precise union of two pieces of hewn wood in a door jamb. His eyes would have been keen enough to discern the difference between just the right piece of wood or stone and that which was merely acceptable. His face would have been deeply lined by years of exposure to the blazing middle Eastern sun.

Here he was, just an ordinary working man, suddenly caught up in a swirling confluence of events and circumstances that apart from God might well have destroyed him. He faced emotional distress — how to deal with the potentially disastrous consequences of an unexpected pregnancy. He faced physical challenges — how to escape the vast military machine unleashed by a jealous king bent on snuffing out the life of Joseph's infant son. Yet, with God, Joseph's faith, courage, compassion, obedience, and strength sustained him. Surely we must see Joseph not as some bit player but as one of God's stars in the unfolding drama of Christmas.

Joseph begins to assume his proper place when one realizes that God spoke directly to him in dreams four times, all of them recorded in Matthew's Gospel. A careful look at each dream will sharpen our appreciation for the man otherwise known simply as "the carpenter of Nazareth."

Call Joseph's first Christmas dream "Embarrassment." God's revealed instruction to Joseph placed him in a potentially embarrassing situation. Capture the message of the first dream in a single sentence: God comes in unexpected ways to unexpected people with unexpected results.

Unexpected Ways

If you look up the word "dream" in the dictionary, you will find it defined as "an illusory experience accepted when it occurs in our sleep, but determined to be unreal as soon as we awake." In fact, the word "dream" derives from a German word which means "to deceive." Little wonder that William Shakespeare calls dreams "the children of an idle brain, begot of nothing but vain fantasy." Such are our human dreams. They arise out of the depths of our own subconscious minds. They are inflamed reflections of our own desires. They are subjective, self-serving, and detached from reality.

Even the Bible is critical of our human dreams. Jeremiah, for example, says, "Speak prophecy, speak truth, speak reality, but leave your dreams at home, for they are like the chaff when compared with the wheat." While our dreams may sometimes reveal truths about our own psychological make-up, they ought not always be understood as God's revealed truth to us.

Yet strangely, surprisingly, unexpectedly, the Bible indicates that God does speak occasionally to His people through dreams. Underscore the word "occasionally." These divine dreams which come from God do not appear often in the Bible. They are clustered in just three places. In Genesis God used dreams to speak to the patriarchs, especially the Old Testament Joseph, as they were building a new life for God's chosen people. God used dreams to speak to Daniel as he envisioned the coming of a new world. Then in Matthew's Christmas story, God used dreams to speak not only to the Wise Men but especially to Joseph.

When you look carefully at those three clusters of divine dreams in Scripture, you discover that when God gets ready to do a new thing in the world, He speaks to His people through dreams. Therefore, when He got ready to do the newest and grandest thing of all—the sending of His Son into the world— God spoke to Joseph through a succession of dreams.

Historically the Jews attached great significance to divine dreams, in part because they were so rare. They understood that God employed such exotic means of communication only in world-changing circumstances. Joseph, the carpenter of Nazareth, would have understood that perfectly. So when he was addressed in his dream as "Son of David," he already would have been open to receiving a remarkable disclosure. Why did the Joseph of the Old Testament and the Joseph of the New Testament receive their revelations in dreams? Couldn't God have chosen a less ambiguous mode of address? Surely God spoke to them in dreams because both Josephs possessed such pure, simple, uncluttered spirituality.

The point is clear. God's dreams are not like our human dreams. His dreams are not illusory. They are not fantasy. They are rooted in reality.

We see that distinctly portrayed in Joseph's first dream. He and Mary were betrothed. The nearest parallel in our own culture would be engagement. But betrothal was much more binding than our custom of engagement. Today couples engage and dis-engage with sometimes flippant ease. There is a pointed story about a fellow who, when he purchased a very expensive engagement ring, asked the jeweler to engrave on the inside of the ring the words: "From Henry to Clara." The jeweler remarked: "Take my advice, son. Have it engraved simply 'From Henry.'" The jeweler's worldly counsel was clearly based on negative experience but, such is the time in which we live.

In Joseph's day, the Jewish marriage procedure included three steps. There was the *engagement*, usually made through parents or through a professional matchmaker when the couple were still young children. Then came *betrothal*, the couple's ratification of the engagement that had been previously arranged. Betrothal lasted one year, resulting in marriage, or ending in divorce. During that year, the couple remained chaste, living in their respective family homes. William Barclay highlights both the nature and permanence of betrothal by stating that a girl whose fiancé died during the year of betrothal was termed in Jewish law "a virgin who is a widow." Then came the *marriage* proper which took place at the end of the year of betrothal.

The Bible says Joseph and Mary were betrothed. Therefore their relationship could be broken only by divorce. That is why Joseph is called "Mary's husband" even before their actual marriage.

So Joseph had made a deep, binding commitment to Mary, and suddenly she told him she was going to have a baby. Can you imagine Joseph's shock and terrible embarrassment?

How it must have been: Joseph, working in his shop, looked up to find two visitors standing there. One was Mary, the other was her father. Their expressions revealed something terribly wrong. Mary's father said, "Joseph, what I am about to say brings no honor to me or to you. Mary, your betrothed, is with child." The words fell upon Joseph like a hammer blow. He felt as if his world were cracking in half and falling beneath him. In shock he cried, "Mary, can this be true?" Through pale, drawn lips she whispered, "Yes, it is true." He felt his knees about to buckle. He felt the muscles twitching in his face as the awful truth threatened to smother him. Unable to respond, he turned away from the two of them, hot tears blinding his eyes. After uncomfortable moments of silence, Mary and her father turned and left the shop.

The next day, after a sleepless night, Joseph arranged a meeting with Mary's father. The law decreed that under such circumstances Mary should be put to death. But Joseph loved her, loved her far too much to think of her being killed or hurt in any way. So Joseph told Mary's father that he would quietly begin divorce proceedings.

Here you begin to catch a first glimpse of the true character of Joseph. While he was terribly hurt, probably even angry, he let the gentle forgiving dimension of his personality hold sway.

While he was caught in this vexing predicament, an angel of the Lord spoke to him in a dream and said: "Joseph, Son of David, do not be afraid to take Mary to be your wife, for it is by the Holy Spirit that she has conceived."

Of all the things Joseph might have expected to hear at that point, "Take Mary to be your wife" was not one of them. In fact, it was exactly the opposite of what he was thinking. He was trying to figure out how to put Mary away, but the dream told him to take her in. He was trying to break off the relationship because of what he and the world would perceive to be her un-holiness, but the dream told him what was happening was the holiest thing the world had yet seen.

This was no fantasy flowing out of his own subconscious mind or his own inflamed desires. This was a clear and specific directive from God: "Take Mary to be your wife." It was an unexpected turn of events that made a shambles out of common sense and his own best thinking. But then, that is often the way God works in our lives. He comes to us in unexpected ways.

I learned that truth at Christmas in 1969. It was a Christmas which would forever change my life.

Trisha and I married in 1964, looking forward eagerly to a full life in the ministry and to a full life at home with children of our own. Three years of seminary and one year of post-graduate work dictated that we postpone having a family. At last, the years of schooling ended, we accepted the call of the First Presbyterian Church of Kilgore, Texas. Not only was life good for us, but we could not imagine it being anything else. It was a feeling which could not, and would not, last. Shortly thereafter, we found to our profound dismay that we would not be able to have children of our own. A dream deferred became a dream destroyed.

We were devastated. We wondered how both our faith and our marriage would survive the shock. We learned a lesson which we have never since forgotten: When we felt that God was so far away, in fact He was never closer. He re-knit the binding ties of love, strengthened the sinews of faith, and set our feet in a new direction: adoption.

After a long process, we were approved as adoptive parents, and there followed a seemingly interminable wait for a child. As the weeks passed into months, we prepared ourselves mentally and emotionally to become parents. Our congregation prepared us materially by providing a crib, diapers, a layette, and all the things a child just days old would need.

Then again the unexpected came to call. On December 18 — it was a Thursday — the adoption agency called to say they had encountered a most unusual situation. They had two little girls who were sisters — would we consider adopting them?

We were stunned into uncomprehending silence. As our minds struggled to digest that piece of news, we were informed that the unusual circumstances required us to spend three days in a relatively distant city so the agency could satisfy itself that the match would work. Then the final shoe dropped: The agency needed an immediate response.

Questions began to cascade over us. On the practical level, how could we possibly leave town for three days so close to Christmas? I had preaching responsibilities not only for Sunday morning, but also for a citywide Christmas candlelight service that Sunday evening. More fundamentally, could we handle it all? Was this really what we had dreamed about and hoped for so long?

We managed to pull ourselves together enough to ask if we could come after the weekend, on Monday, Tuesday, and Wednesday, even though that Wednesday would be Christmas Eve. The agency agreed. This unexpected event had come crashing into our well-ordered lives, and because we were not sure it would work out, we could share our dilemma with no one. We threw ourselves upon the limitless resources of God. He stayed with us on our emotional roller coaster: excitement, frustration, fear, happiness — all were there in double measure. The sermon I preached that Sunday night (even though prepared weeks in advance) was built around my imaginings of what Joseph and Mary must have felt during that First Christmas. The words were delivered out of a churning mind and heart.

The next day, Monday, we made the three-hour trip for our initial meeting with the little girls, one almost 2 years old and the other, 6 months. As we took them into our arms for the first time, most of our questions vanished. We both sensed the intention of God, so clear it might as well have been written on the wall: "I have chosen these children for you and you for them. Take them to your home and to your heart."

Tuesday, we informed our families and our friends at the church that we had not just one child but two, Meg and Beth, and that we would be bringing them home the next day — Christmas Eve!

We then set out on our return journey, with nothing for the children except the clothes on their backs, and nothing for ourselves except a sudden rush of anxiety about being parents. Thankfully, Meg and Beth, lulled by the sound of the car engine, dropped off to sleep. Trisha and I did not say a word for the next couple of hours, ostensibly because we did not wish to wake the children, but actually because fear had put our brains in overdrive and choked off our ability to speak.

Nearing home, our anxiety turned to semi-controlled panic. What were we going to do? The things we had prepared at home were designed for an infant — and for only one infant at that. And Christmas? It had been pushed so far into the background that we agreed to simply forego it that year.

Then as we turned the corner toward home we saw welcoming signs all over the house. We stepped inside to encounter the most astonishing outpouring of love we had ever known. The people in the church had added a youth bed to the nursery, swapped and doubled much of the clothing, stocked the kitchen with food, purchased a wonderland of toys, and placed wrapped presents for all of us under the Christmas tree. Trisha and I stood in the midst of this incredible scene, each cradling a new daughter in our arms, and wept with joy for a God and a people who love like that.

Every Christmas Eve I relive those precious moments, and every time I weep tears of joy. It is God's annual reminder to me that He comes to us in unexpected ways and makes a shambles out of common sense and our own best thinking. But then that is part of the reason I love Him so.

Unexpected People

What was so unexpected at the First Christmas was not the announcement that the Messiah was coming; the Jews had been eagerly awaiting the arrival of a Saviour for centuries. There was nothing shocking or unexpected about the notion that the Messiah was on the way. Nor was there anything shocking or unexpected about the way He would come. The Jewish believers of that day fully expected the Messiah to come on clouds of glory surrounded by legions of attending angels. People comfortable with the idea of God's arranging that kind of cosmic spectacle would not have been shocked by something as comparatively simple as a virgin birth.

No, what was so shocking, so unexpected, so unnerving, so downright embarrassing was that the Lord of the universe, the Saviour of the world, the Messiah of God would be entrusted to the care of a teenaged girl and an unknown carpenter from an obscure village. That was the scandal! That was the embarrassment! That was the unexpectedness of it all—not that it was going to happen, not even how it was going to happen, but that it was going to happen to "nobodies" like Mary and Joseph.

Life for Joseph at this point was one jolt following another. No sooner had he recovered from the shock of Mary's expectancy than he was jolted again with the news that the two of them would be required to travel from Nazareth to their ancestral home, the little town of Bethlehem, in order to participate in the Roman census. The journey from Nazareth to Bethlehem was never easy in those days, but given their particular circumstances, the journey must have been excruciating. The ninety-mile trip took them east to the Jordan River valley, south along the flatlands beside the river, a turn to the west at Jericho, up and over the hills of the Judean wilderness to Jerusalem, then on the few miles to Bethlehem. Under normal conditions they could have made twenty miles a day, but given Mary's situation they would have been lucky to make ten miles a day. The last stretch of the journey, through the Judean wilderness, was especially tough. The desert can be a harsh and unforgiving place. Not only that, but the wilderness brought with it the constant threat of attack by outlaws. Combine the hardness of the journey, the harshness of the conditions, and the hazards of the circumstances, and you begin to appreciate what a mammoth challenge Joseph had to face in transporting Mary to Bethlehem. Here we begin to catch a glimpse of how Joseph met the challenges life set before him by throwing himself in absolute dependence upon the power of God.

Do not then miss what Joseph's Christmas dream is all about—that the most important thing in the world can happen to the least important people in the world—that the King of kings and the Lord of lords can take up residence in the most ordinary of lives—that the greatest Somebody who ever lived can come to nobodies like Joseph, like Mary, like you, like me.

Some words of Dietrich Bonhoeffer, the German theologian murdered by the Nazis, seem appropriate here: "Christ is among us as we gather together even with all of our differences. And it is when we are together that we frequently discover Christ through other people."[1]

Let me put that same truth in another way. During the last World War, on a desolate battlefield in France, where all the houses and the trees were leveled and where there was nothing but yellow mud and the stench of death— as night fell over the "no man's land" separating the American lines from the forces of the enemy, there was a silencing of the guns and the sound of an awful calm. Then, out of the darkness, came a voice calling, "Help! Help!" The words were in English. It was an American soldier. Evidently, he had been wounded and knocked unconscious, but now the coolness of the evening roused him. He didn't know where he was or what to do. He could not move. So he called out in agony and in pain: "Help! Help!" For a long moment, nothing happened. Then, suddenly on the German lines, a bright light was turned on. A German soldier shined the light onto his own face and waved a white flag. He then walked out into that "no man's land," a perfect target, and searched until he found the wounded G.I. He bent down, picked up the boy, and carried him to the American side. There he put the wounded soldier into the arms of his American buddies. The German did not say a word. He simply looked at those American soldiers, lifted his hand and made the sign of the cross, and then went back to his own lines again. Yes, we need to remember that God does come to the most unexpected people in unexpected ways, and that means that God can come to the likes of you and me.

Unexpected Results

Think about Joseph. Joseph had not sought the celestial limelight. He was a simple carpenter; he could not even be termed "an artist with wood." In those days carpenters worked not only with wood but also with stone, and their work was less creative than functional. They would cut trees into boards and chip stones into great blocks, and they would fashion them into walls, support beams, and roofs for houses, or yokes, plows, and wagons for farming. Joseph was not so much an artisan as a day-laborer, a frightfully ordinary man for the extraordinary responsibility God was assigning to him.

"Joseph's Lullaby," a perfectly lovely little song written by Marcy Heisler and John Kavanaugh, dares to crawl into Joseph's head, seeking to discern his thoughts on that First Christmas. Here is a portion of the song:

> Mary, are you sleeping?
> Mary, I'm afraid.
> Mary can I live up to
> The choice that God has made?
> Jesus, can You tell me,
> Here upon my knee,
> What kind of father will I be?

How it must have been: Joseph wondered what kind of father he would be. He was just a carpenter. He knew only how to work with wood. How could he be expected to train a child to become the Saviour of the world? Surely some mistake had been made. Joseph shared his fears with Mary. She replied to him, "Joseph, God made no mistake. You are a craftsman with wood. You take green trees that are twisted and make them into beams that are straight and strong. You take rough timbers and smooth them into beauty. And you love to fix broken things – you love to make them like new again. God made no mistake, Joseph, when He chose you to raise His Son, for what you have learned to do with wood, the Saviour of the world must learn to do with men."

Mary's words surely would have been soothing, but Joseph must still have struggled to grasp it all. He couldn't foresee what it would all mean. He could not have imagined how the rough boards of the child's first bed prefigured another crude frame that would bear His weight. He could not know that the baby would be born in Bethlehem – the City of David — and die in Jerusalem –David's City. Joseph could not foresee that between those two points, all the people who would take Jesus into their hearts, a whole world's worth, would be lifted to glory.

Joseph could not begin to understand any of that — at least not on that First Christmas. He was in no way uniquely prepared or equipped to be the earthly father of the Son of God. He had not asked for the Messiah to come to him. He had not volunteered Mary to be the mother. He had not done anything. But suddenly the angel appeared, declaring: "When you take Mary, you will be getting the Christ as well."

It happens still. How many people have found Christ through their spouse? How many people have found Christ through their mother or their father? How many people have found Christ because of a humble Sunday School teacher or an obscure pastor whose name is forgotten? How many people have found Christ because He was living so beautifully in some ordinary, unexpected person?

My own experience reflects that very basic truth. Time and again God has brought into my life unexpected surprises and revelations of His truth through unexpected people. Let me introduce you to just three of them.

There is Heyward McDonald. As a graduate of the United States Naval Academy, he was rising rapidly through the Navy's chain of command. One day, accidentally, he was innoculated with an unsterilized needle. He contracted polio and lost the use of his legs. The bright promise of his naval career was washed away, but he refused to let that swamp his spirit. He learned to live with crutches and a wheelchair ... and he altered the direction of his life. He went to law school and eventually entered politics in South Carolina. Understand: In order to climb stairs, he must turn around backwards and with the strength of his arms pressing down against his crutches, carefully lever his useless legs back and up for each step. Political experts advised: "No one who has to back up the stairs can get elected." That did not stop him. He ran, and he was elected. He has gone on to become one of the most powerful, influential, and admired figures in the public service of his state.

Here is how McDonald reflects upon his life today: "Polio paralyzed my legs but not my heart. I am a better man and I am a stronger Christian because of this disease." When you allow Heyward McDonald to take a place in your heart, you get Christ, too.

There is Daniel Berry. Blind since early childhood, he is now an ordained Presbyterian minister of unusual effectiveness. When I asked him to preach in the church I was serving in Arkansas, he said to me before worship, "Take me into the sanctuary." I did. He then asked "Are there columns in this room?"

"Yes," I replied.

"Take me to one of them." He then pressed his chest up against the column and stretched his arms as far around it as he could reach. In that position he quickly calculated in his computer-like mind the length of that sanctuary.

He commented, "I need to do that in order to properly use my voice and in order to have good eye-contact with the congregation." Remember he is blind, but he said, "You know a preacher has got to have good eye-contact with the people."

Later that morning as he stood to preach, a blind man helping others to see Jesus, I thought to myself, "When you let Daniel Berry into your heart, you get Christ as well." By the way, we measured the sanctuary later; he missed it by nine inches!

There is Kim Lee Shin. He lives at the Wilson Leprosy Center in Soonchun, Korea. The ravages of leprosy have left him with no toes, no fingers, no hands, no ears, no eyes, no nose, no facial features... nothing but a smile. Every day he assembles fifteen other blind lepers in what is called "Scripture House" — one room, four walls, no furnishings, just a pad on the floor. For four hours each day they play the harmonica and sing gospel songs; they pray for their fellow lepers and their missionary doctors; and they memorize Scripture. That's right ...they memorize Scripture...by listening over and over and over to God's Word on audio tapes. They have completed the New Testament and are better than one-third through the Old Testament. The day Trisha and I visited the Scripture House, Kim Lee Shin asked us to pick a passage of the New Testament for them to recite. "Any passage," he instructed. "Just pick one from the top of your head." I chose Mark, Chapter 7.

Kim Lee Shin delivered the choice to his friends. On cue they began to speak as one voice. Trisha and I listened, minds awestruck, eyes tear-filled, as they recited word for word the seventh chapter of the Gospel of Mark. Mark it down: If you let Kim Lee Shin into your heart, he will bring Christ with him.

It is the most amazing, the most surprising, the most unexpected fact of human experience that those people who know their own weaknesses, their own limitations, their own helplessness, their own powerlessness—those people are the ones who end up strong. Those people who know that they cannot go it alone through life and therefore throw themselves into the arms of the Saviour—they are the ones who in the end are triumphant and victorious.

It does not matter how worthless or insignificant or unimportant we may feel. The message of Joseph's first Christmas dream is that we are of infinite value to God. We are the objects of His seeking, saving love. He comes to us in the form of Jesus, who was born to Mary and Joseph, and who lived and grew only to die in order that you and I might have life. God does come in *unexpected* ways to *unexpected* people with *unexpected* results.

Amazing! Joseph never spoke a word in the Christmas story, but what he *did* speaks volumes. God said to him in a dream, "Take Mary to be your wife. Take her into your home and into your heart, not because she needs a husband, but because she has the Christ." The Bible says that Joseph obeyed the Christmas dream. He took Jesus into his home and into his heart.

I invite you to do the same.

∽ DREAM TWO ∾

BANISHMENT

It actually happened in a church I know...

A worried mother phoned the church office on the afternoon before the Sunday School Christmas pageant to say that her small son, who was to play the role of Joseph in the pageant, had caught the flu and was confined to bed. The teacher replied: "Well, it is too late to get another Joseph, so we will just have to write him out of the script." So they did... and very few of those who watched the play realized that the cast was incomplete.

Joseph, the carpenter of Nazareth, is the silent, forgotten figure of the Christmas story. We could never think of Christmas without singing angels, bright-eyed shepherds, regal Wise Men, a harried innkeeper, and even villainous Herod. We could never have Christmas without them. But Joseph? Too often, we write him out of the script. No longer. Joseph obviously understood the vocabulary of God. When God spoke, Joseph not only heard, he listened and responded. We see that clearly in his second Christmas dream. I call it "Banishment." The message of the dream is that the real story of Christmas involves rejection, protection, and direction. Take them one at a time.

Rejection

Christmas points to realities that are not very secure in a world like ours. That is made clear in the second chapter of Matthew. After the Wise Men came, worshipped the infant King, offered their gifts, and went on their way, an angel appeared to Joseph in a dream saying: "Get up, take the child and his mother, and escape to Egypt. Stay there until I tell you, for Herod is going to search for the child to kill him."

At that point Joseph did not have to worry so much about Mary or the Wise Men or the shepherds. The circle of his concern was narrowed to just that child, that precious jewel, that emblem of future hope. Herod was seeking to destroy the child, and the threat was terrifyingly real. The angel in the dream sounded the alarm to Joseph, and with that instant obedience to God so typical of Joseph, he rose, took the child and the child's mother, and by night departed to Egypt, there to remain until further notice.

The flight into Egypt is a jarring note in the Christmas story. King Herod was rattled by a helpless baby. Usually kings are troubled by malcontents breeding insurrection or by diminishing popularity or by alien armies massing troops along the border. Yet here was King Herod troubled by a child newly born.

History remembers this monster as "Herod the Great." What a dreadful misnomer! He was king of Judea both by law and in fact, yet he was not at all secure in that position. He was vulnerable, as all of us are, to anyone who could do a better job; but he was more vulnerable than most. There was little good in the man. A sly, cunning, crafty old fox, he ruled on the basis of deceit and cruelty. The blood of many murdered people, including his own wife and at least two of his sons, stained his hands. Both physical and moral violence marked his every day and his every decision. As a matter of fact, in order to be certain that there would be a public mourning on the day of his death, he ordered to be arrested and detained in prison a large group of Jewish people with instruction that at the moment he died they were to be killed as well, thus plunging the land into grief. That should give you an idea as to the kind of man he was. To think that anyone could consider such a malignant figure Herod the Great!

Needless to say, Herod's subjects so hated him that rumors constantly circulated about attempts to overthrow him. Whenever the rumors reached his ears, they never failed to trouble him. Matthew writes of this latest rumor: " When King Herod heard this he was disturbed and all Jerusalem with him." Ernest T. Campbell claims that just as "a tyrannical father can put a whole family on edge, so an agitated king can set a whole town to seething." Herod was agitated, and Jerusalem seethed.

What a topsy-turvy experience that First Christmas was! Wise Men had come bowing in worship and bearing gifts for the child, then suddenly, an angel appeared with urgent news: "Herod is out to kill this baby!" The Magi had sought the infant King to crown Him; now Herod was seeking the infant King to destroy Him. It was hard enough to comprehend that the Wise Men would travel months and months across desert wastes to worship and adore the Messiah. It must have been even harder to comprehend how Herod, without even investigating, would slaughter innocent children in an attempt to destroy a perceived rival. Yes, as great as was the mystery of the visit of the Wise Men, even greater was the mystery of the malignancy in Herod's heart.

Joseph knew all about Herod and his capacity for indescribable savagery. Jolted into action by Herod's threat, and shielded under the cover of darkness, Joseph took his family and headed for the Egyptian border. It was not far. Sixty miles. Even with an infant, they could make it in 24 hours of hard traveling. Reaching the border would guarantee them safety from Herod, leaving a long hazardous trip on to the city of Cairo. No miracles now. No bands of singing angels. Just fear and hard work. They had to pack up the inventory of the infant King and flee through the darkness like common criminals. In one moment, they were warmed by the adoring attention of shepherds and Wise Men; in the next moment, they were chilled by the midnight wind blowing over trackless Sinai sands. Only days earlier they had been dazzled by exquisite gifts of gold, frankincense and myrrh. Now those selfsame gifts would have to be used to sustain their flight from a jealous, murderous king. Christmas ... what a topsy-turvy thing...what a muddle of mysteries for Joseph to unravel!

In this second dream, Joseph discovered a disconcerting truth: No sooner had Jesus Christ entered the world than efforts were made to banish Him from the face of the earth. Christ drew deadly opposition from the very beginning. The shadow of the cross fell even over His manger.

Christmas has trouble in it now just as it had trouble then. The selfish do not like to hear a message about a God who loved the world so much that He gave His only Son. The selfish build their lives on getting, not on giving, so Christmas is an offense to them. The cruel do not want to hear about the kindness and compassion and mercy of God shown at Christmas. The cruel want to dominate, to intimidate, to manipulate people, and it infuriates them to hear that at the center of the universe is a loving Christ. Those consumed by achieving success in the world's terms, those lusting for the things that money can buy, and the power and prestige that go with it all—they are put off by Christmas.

The message of Christmas is that ultimately none of those things is important. The most important things in life are faith and family and friendship and caring and sharing. Not for Herod. When Herod heard what happened in Bethlehem he was enraged. Immediately this aging, raging ruler set out to destroy Jesus. Heaven help us, there are those today who have let evil take control of their lives, and they do not want to hear the Christmas message any more than Herod did.

Christmas is not just twinkling stars, lovely songs, angelic choirs, lavish gifts. Christmas is also about a midnight flight over desert wastes into exile in Egypt. "He came to His own and His own received Him not." Or as the old carol puts it, "We didn't know who He was." That is part of the Christmas story—rejection.

Protection

Christmas points to securities made real by a God like ours. The angel said to Joseph in the dream: "Flee to Egypt for there you will be safe and secure." Of course, it was not so unusual that Joseph would choose to try to escape with his family to

Egypt. Egypt had long been a place of refuge for threatened people. Jacob and his sons went there to keep from starving to death during famine in Israel. When Jeroboam was trying to get away from Solomon, he fled to Egypt. When Uriah was running away from Jehoiachim, he escaped to Egypt. Egypt was the Switzerland of that day—once you crossed its borders, you would be safe from outside influence. Egypt offered refuge, shelter, security, protection. In fact, because Egypt had long been a sanctuary from troubles in Judea, a sizable number of Jewish refugees resided there. For the Holy Family it would have been as close to home as they could get and yet not be home.

Some people try to move through life with a false bravado. They say: "Defeat is not in my vocabulary. The word 'retreat' never crosses my lips. I am always upbeat and positive. I do not allow anything or anyone to get the best of me." Let me assert that I am an active proponent and practitioner of the power of positive thinking. It is one of the secrets of truly significant living. However, there are times of setback in life, times of suffering, times of sorrow, times when you have to flee, times when you have to beat a strategic retreat, times when you cannot win, no matter how hard you try, no matter how positively you think. Joseph understood that, so he sought the protection of God for his family and himself. Off they went to Egypt.

Note that they were not told how long they would have to stay. The angel's instructions are so interesting: "Flee to Egypt and remain there till I tell you." Catch that. God was saying to Joseph: "Look, I am not going to guarantee you any quick, easy answers. I am not even going to tell you how long you will have to stay in Egypt. I am asking you to believe that I will be protecting you. I will be watching over you. I will be looking after you. I will be your guardian angel. You will be safe and secure in Egypt. One day there will be a sequel to this mad flight. One day there will be another dream, and I will tell you that Herod is no longer a threat and that you can go home. In the meantime, you need only to believe that I will be with you."

Do you see what that means? It means that we never encounter an "Egypt-experience" in our lives, we never encounter
the sting of setback but that the Lord is there. There is never a
darkened home, never a sore temptation, never a broken heart,
never a painful decision, never an open grave, but that the Lord
is there to guard us, protect us, sustain us, even strengthen us.
Oft-times people emerge from exile stronger from the experience.

That was true in biblical times. Paul, after his dramatic con-
version on the Damascus Road, entered into a period of self-
imposed exile. He captures it in just a few words written to the
Galatians: "I went away into Arabia." That was Paul's "Egypt-
experience." It may have lasted just a few months or as long as
ten years. We cannot be sure. However, we can be sure that it
was a time for him to decide who he was and whose he was —
a time for him to prepare his mind, heart, body, and spirit for
the demanding challenges that lay ahead. He returned from
exile possessing all the tools he needed to become both the
Church's grandest theologian and her greatest missionary.

John, the disciple Jesus specially loved, was exiled in his
latter years to the island of Patmos. Those years marked John's
"Egypt-experience." There, John — the man Jesus once labeled
a "son of thunder" — was softened into the "disciple of love"
and was given the triumphant, apocalyptic vision we know as
The Revelation to John. Patmos proved to be a place of strengthening for him.

The same is true in our own time. Think of modern leaders
who have had an "Egypt-experience." Franklin Roosevelt. His
political star was rising, and he became the vice-presidential
candidate of the Democratic Party. Then suddenly, crippling
polio sent him to Campobello for several long years. Campobello
was FDR's Egypt. There, this pathetic, helpless man, who had
to drag his withered legs behind him, was strengthened and
prepared for a presidency that would leave a lasting mark upon
America.

Winston Churchill. In 1928, he was First Lord of the Admiralty, heir-apparent to the Prime Ministry. Then in 1929, he lost everything: his job, his party, his fortune. There followed ten long wilderness years. Egypt. But he came back stronger than when he left.

Aleksandr Solzhenitsyn. The courage of his convictions caused the Soviet Communist authorities in his native Russia first to sentence him to an internal exile in the Siberian Gulag, and then to banish him completely from his homeland in 1972. The years of exile, an unending Egypt-experience, carved deep lines of suffering into his face, but they sharpened the power of his pen and honed a razor's edge to his moral and prophetic voice. Some call him "the greatest figure of the 20th century." Solzhenitsyn himself looked back upon the exile and declared, "I was lucky to have been in the camps. They gave me an understanding of Soviet life I could not have had otherwise."

God, in the same manner, strengthened and sustained the Holy Family in Egypt. Bishop Fulton Sheen once said: "During the First Christmas the Exodus was reversed as Jesus made Egypt His temporary home." How true. The very land which had been a land of bondage and pain for God's people became a place of refuge and safety for God's Son.

How it must have been: Joseph, still brimming with the happiness of holding the infant Jesus in his arms, was abruptly brought back to grim reality. In what would be more properly termed a nightmare than a dream, the angel alerted Joseph to Herod's designs on Jesus. Without even waiting for the dawn's early light, Joseph roused his sleeping family, packed their provisions, including the gifts of the Magi, and set out on the highway south. The journey to Egypt was far more ambitious than that which led from Nazareth to Bethlehem, and was more than twice as long. Undoubtedly they took the regular caravan trail from Bethlehem to Hebron, turned sharply west to Gaza, and then followed the coastal highway down to the Egyptian border. The journey would have been physically taxing because of its length and emotionally draining because of the ever-present threat of danger. Here is one more revealing portrait of Joseph: A considerate, protective, resourceful, courageous, mature individual — a truly good man — managing the difficult and hazardous journey to Egypt.

It is no accident, I think, that the oldest organized church in Christendom is the Coptic Church in Egypt. The years when the Holy Family was banished to Egypt were not idle years. Wonderful stories of what happened during those years are part of the Coptic tradition. I remember, for example, visiting St. Sergius' Church in Cairo and being shown the spot where, according to tradition, an Egyptian family sheltered the Holy Family.

Or there is the lovely story from the same tradition that tells how Joseph and Mary and Jesus, during their escape into Egypt, took refuge in a cave. It was very cold, so cold that the ground was white with frost. A little spider saw the baby Jesus and wished that he could do something to keep the child warm. He decided to do the only thing he could do: spin a heavy web across the doorway to the cave. Later, a detachment of Herod's soldiers, searching for the refugee family, spotted the cave. When the squadron commander saw the spider's web, he declared, "No one is in there, for anyone entering would have torn the web." The soldiers moved on, leaving the Holy Family safe, all because a little spider spun his web across the entryway. By the way, the tradition tells us that the tinsel streamers we place on our Christmas trees today represent the strands of the spider's web glistening with that silver frost.

These traditional stories rising out of the Coptic Church in Egypt have about them an underlying truth. The sojourn in Egypt was a time when the Holy Family experienced the protection and the provision of God. The hazards of refugee life bound ever more tightly the ties of love between Joseph and Mary and their first-born child. The exile in Egypt forged the steely-strength that Mary and Joseph would need for the difficulties they would face later in life. The fact that Jesus spent His earliest years in a land not His own, accepted by people not His own, helped to shape His consuming passion for all the world's people—not just His own. All because of God's protection.

In this hazardous, hurtful world, do not let setbacks set you back. Cling to the knowledge that you are kept by God in every situation and circumstance.

That is what David Redding avowed when he told the story of a little girl named Suzanne. The child was being carried by her mother out of their village, devastated by the movement of armies across France in the final days of the Second World War. Homes were gone. Places of business were leveled. The town was ruined. It was like a wilderness — there was nothing left. They paused for a moment at the place where once the town hall had stood. Suddenly Suzanne's mother stopped in her tracks. There, forcing its way up through the rubble, was a rose bush, and it was in full bloom! "Look, Suzanne," her mother cried. "Remember that a rose can grow anywhere."[2]

Hold onto that; hold onto it for dear life. Out of life's rubble, out of life's setbacks, out of life's "Egypt-experiences," because of Jesus Christ, something beautiful can and will emerge. Part of the Christmas story: protection.

Direction

Christmas points to the Lord who directs lives like yours and like mine. Joseph's second Christmas dream reminds us that the people of this world are in one of two camps. Either they love Jesus, or they hate Him. Either they are for Him, or they are against Him. Either they live their lives under His direction, or they don't. Some say legions of people are neutral on the issue. They are indifferent. They do not care one way or another. But neutrality and indifference are just subtle forms of opposition. The great hymn underscores the truth: "At the name of Jesus every knee shall bow/ Every tongue confess Him King of Glory now." But that was not true on the First Christmas, and it is not true today.

Why? I think the answer can be found in some remarkable words Paul wrote to the Corinthians: "God chose that which is foolish in the world to shame the wise. God chose that which is weak in the world to shame the strong. God chose things that cannot be, in order to bring to nothing the things that are." Baffling words at first glance, but further reflection reveals that Paul was saying that earthly power, whether regal or personal, political or financial, social or psychological— earthly power is temporary. In the end, it is meaningless. It is worthless. If you do not believe that, take another look at King Herod.

The power of Jesus Christ is something quite different. It is the glory of our Lord Jesus Christ that He takes the lives of those who do not seem too prominent in the earthly scheme and transforms them into nothing other than the sons and daughters of Almighty God. He gives to those who get no respect a sense of self-respect. He offers to those who have little hope in life the gift of eternal life. He tells those who in the eyes of the world are worthless that in the eyes of God they are worth the life of God's own Son. He takes those who are set running in fear and defeat and surrounds them with the protective mantle of His grace. Get the point? Jesus Christ, meager child, manger-born, is nothing less than the most powerful, most uplifting, most ennobling, most enabling force ever turned loose in the world.

The Bethlehem cradle rocked King Herod back on his heels. Give Herod credit for being smart enough to realize that what he was about and what Jesus was about could not peacefully co-exist in the same world. One of them had to go. Of course that is why on Good Friday the people cried, "Give us Barabbas. We would rather have him loose than Jesus." That is why Pontius Pilate stooped to washing his hands of Jesus, never lifting a finger to save Him. That is why the message of the Cradle-child rocks kings and other agents of power even in our day, whether their power derives from politics or economics or just an inflated ego. That is why the message of Christ's Church so discomforts those who put their trust in their own resources rather than in the resources of God. That is why nativity scenes in public places and little children singing Christmas carols in school are such a threat to some people.

It seems foolish that the simple story of a baby born to peasant parents should strike fear in so many hearts. It seems foolish that the lovely, lifting, lilting, lasting beauty of Christmas carols should trouble so many people. Paul was right. God takes what is foolish and uses it to shame the wise. God takes a weak and helpless child and uses Him to shame a power-hungry king.

Wrap your heart around this: Christmas is more than sticky-sweet sentimentalism, more than a frivolous birthday party, more than a harmless myth to be tolerated like a Mother Goose rhyme. Christmas is a choice. Do not go shopping and singing your way through Christmas without realizing that in the final analysis Christmas means coming to this decision in your life: Either you are for Jesus or you are against Him. Herod made his decision. He knew that he and Jesus could not exist together. One of them had to go. Herod tried to stop Jesus, but he could not do it.

Frankly that is why I am not terribly concerned about the concerted effort by some to transform Christmas into just another secular holiday. Jesus cannot be stopped. Ban all the nativity scenes, Christmas carols, and references to Jesus you wish. It will not stop Him. It did not work in the days of King Herod. It will not work now.

Did you know that Helen Keller never went to church in her early childhood? She was deaf; she was blind; she could not speak. She had no opportunity to learn the story of God revealed in Jesus Christ. Then she was taken to visit Phillips Brooks, the greatest preacher America has ever produced. Through her teacher he told her in the simplest possible language how God had sent Jesus of Nazareth to show His love, to teach His will, to make Himself known to us. As he told the story, Helen Keller's face lit up and she spelled out into the palm of her interpreter's hand this sentence: "I knew all the time that there must be someone like that; I just didn't know His name was Jesus." The experience changed the direction of her life, and she became a radiant witness to our Lord. When Jesus catches hold of you, He gives your life a sense of direction.

Here's the bottom line…

Do you know His name? Christmas means coming to a decision about Jesus Christ in your life. Learn His name. Love His name. Claim His name as your own. Take Him into your home and into your heart … NOW!

∽ DREAM THREE ∽

POSTPONEMENT

Just north of Chicago, there is a town called Oak Brook. In that town, there is a church called Christ Church. In that church, there is a chapel called The Chapel of the Carpenter.

What is so unusual about that chapel is that it is built around an actual carpenter's shop that once stood in Nazareth. The shop was carefully and completely disassembled, shipped over here, and then just as carefully re-assembled in its original form. Once that was done, the chapel was built around it. When you stand in that chapel and look at that carpenter's shop from Nazareth, you are struck with its simplicity, its poverty, its earthiness. There is nothing about it that is extraordinary. But I suppose that is why it seems such an apt memorial to Joseph. For Joseph, the carpenter of Nazareth, was simple and poor and earthy and not at all extraordinary.

However, what happened to Joseph was extraordinary. Joseph was responsible for the welfare of God's only begotten Son. Joseph, God's special agent-in-charge, was diligent to the task. During the day his energy was so focused upon the needs of his family that anything unrelated dropped off the screen of his attention. During the night his spirit was so alert to the divine signals that God could speak to him in his dreams. Night and day, every other consideration in his life assumed secondary importance to the safety of this Holy Child.

By God's grace such faithful and devoted servants, keepers of the faith, have never been wanting in the world. Even when the powers of darkness have sought to extinguish the light of the Gospel, these guardians of belief have banked the flame and kept it burning. Their patron saint is a simple, down-to-earth, hardworking carpenter from Nazareth named Joseph.

A third time God spoke a clear word of instruction to Joseph through a dream. The dream can be described by the word: "Postponement." The message of the dream is that Christmas is a time for both bad news and Good News.

The Bad News of Christmas

In Matthew 2:19 we read: "After Herod died, an angel of the Lord appeared in a dream to Joseph in Egypt and said, 'Get up, take the child and his mother and go to the land of Israel for those who were trying to take the child's life are dead.'"

Focus, please, on the words, "Herod died." Remember what it means for Herod to die as part of the Christmas story. We tend to think of Christmas as being about birth, the beginning of life. Of course, it is. But it is also about death, the end of life. The Bible says, "Herod died." The evil king was finished. The Bible also says, "...those who were trying to take the child's life are dead." I call that "the plural of influence." Not only Herod, but the whole system he inspired and all the people who jumped to do his bidding — that whole web of evil — was gone. The angel was saying that God's judgment had prevailed. "The wages of sin is death," and Herod's demise was unmistakable proof.

Herod let evil take control of his life. He put down all opposition with ruthless severity. He even dealt harshly with his own family. His insecurity and his lust for power consumed him. Once, to please his wife Mariamne, he appointed her brother high priest. But when her brother achieved some popularity, a threatened Herod had him put to death. Mariamne never forgave him for that, and so finally, in a fit of rage, Herod ordered her execution, too.

That was the real turning point in Herod's life. While he was no paragon of virtue beforehand, the murder of his wife started the downward spiral that ended in the total disintegration of his character. Formerly, like Shakespeare's Macbeth, Herod killed for the sake of expediency; now he killed just for the sake of killing. Formerly, he distrusted only his enemies;

now he distrusted everyone. With no pangs of conscience at all, he executed at least two of his sons. The Romans even had a joke about it in the form of a Latin play on words. Since Jewish dietary laws prohibited the eating of pork, the Romans joked, "It is better to be Herod's *huios* than to be Herod's *hios;*" that is, "It is better to be Herod's pig than to be Herod's son."

In the failed attempt to snuff out the life of Jesus, the blood-thirsty Herod committed the most infamous of all his hideous deeds. He slaughtered the innocent children in Bethlehem. Once more death intrudes on the Christmas story.

If you were to travel to Bethlehem today and stand in Manger Square, you would see two churches sharing a common wall, built over the site where Christ was born. If you were to descend the stairs in one of the churches, you would see the cave-stable and the place where the manger held the newborn King. If you were then to descend the stairs of the other church, you would see the spot where the children murdered by King Herod are buried. Think of that. The people of Bethlehem chose to bury those children immediately adjacent to the spot where the angels sang and the shepherds knelt in worship before the infant Saviour. Birthplace and burial crypt, side-by-side.

It is worth remembering what actually happened. I have read suggestions that the number of babies slain was in the hundreds or even thousands. However, archaeological evidence shows us rather conclusively that the population in the region of Bethlehem at that time numbered about one thousand. Demographic studies from that period reveal that the annual birth-rate was about thirty per one thousand. That means there would have been some sixty children in that region under two years of age, with half that number being male. While the murdered children did not number in hundreds or thousands, even the massacre of thirty young children injects a note of revulsion into the sweetness of the Christmas story. I find myself unable to celebrate Christmas without remembering those little babies and their devastated parents in Bethlehem.

Surely those children were the first Christian martyrs, the first ones to die for the sake of Jesus. They died for Him so that He might live on this earth. Later on, He died for them so that they might have eternal life. I believe they occupy a special place in heaven. Just as they were buried then beside the spot where Jesus was born, I believe they are now at His side in Glory.

Sadly for Herod, there was only the inevitable judgment of God. He died a lonely, horrible death, wracked with violent pain. We know the details from ancient historians, and they are too gruesome to discuss in polite company. When at last this vile and loathsome ruler stopped breathing, at that moment, his whole kingdom breathed a sigh of relief. As one historian noted: "For all the official pomp at Herod's funeral, there was not a trace of sorrow." The judgment of God prevailed. But then the judgment of God always prevails. Sooner or later, God will shiver a sinful life into ruins. God may not balance the books at the end of the week or the month or the year, but God does always balance the books.

While I wish I did not have to mention this bad news in the Christmas story, it is there and we need to be aware of it. The sins of Herod are in us all—not as extreme perhaps, but they are there. Sin is a reality, even at Christmas. We do not like to think about that; but then it is always hard for us to face the reality of sin in our own lives, so we joke about it. Someone reported this bit of graffiti on the New York subway: "We didn't invent sin. We're just trying to perfect it." Then there was the billboard that appeared one day and had upon it this message in big block letters: "Tired of sin? Call 876-1952." Some clever soul proceeded to take a can of spray paint and put under it this line: "If you're not, call 971-3582."

We can joke about our sins, but they will not go away. According to Martin of Tours: "The ultimate proof of the sinner is that he will not admit his own sin." Thomas Carlyle wrote: "The greatest fault is to be conscious of none." Isaiah put it this way: "All we like sheep have gone astray; we have turned everyone to his own way." Like it or not, Christmas confronts us with the reality of our sins and with the reality of God's judgment upon evil.

The Christmas story contains both the manger and the massacre to remind us that there is a struggle going on within us. The evil that is within us will do anything to destroy the good that is within us. Once we surrender, even slightly, to that evil, it will seize control and destroy the good. That is precisely what happened to Herod. He sent his troops to Bethlehem and tried to kill the greatest good the world has ever known. Futile effort. He never found Jesus, but he did find judgment. Bad news for Herod. Joseph heard the news from the angel: "…Herod died … those who were trying to take the child's life are dead."

The Good News of Christmas

Look again at Matthew 2:19: "…an angel of the Lord appeared in a dream to Joseph in Egypt and said 'Get up, take the child and his mother and go to the land of Israel…'" Call it "Second Exodus." As Moses was called out of Egypt to save the people of Israel from the bondage of slavery, so Jesus was called out of Egypt in His infancy, through the divine message given to Joseph, to save humankind from the bondage of sin.

Focus on the words "…go to the land of Israel…" How interesting that the angel used the name Israel. Understand that Israel was not the geographical name of that place in the time of Jesus. It was known then as Palestine. The angel carefully chose the name Israel to bring to mind the Old Testament idea of a land of promise. The angel meant not so much a geographical location as a state of mind.

Here then is the message the angel delivered: "Joseph, Herod is dead, but the ultimate victory is still a long way off. It is postponed, delayed, deferred. It will come, but not yet. There is still much to be done, and it will not be easy. This child still has a long way to go and a long way to grow. Take the child and go where there is hope, where there is promise, where there is the expectation of the coming of the Kingdom of God. Be patient, but be hopeful. Ultimately, God's promise of salvation will be fulfilled. In time, your hope will be rewarded with victory."

How it must have been: Joseph, it is reasonable to assume, had been born in Bethlehem since that was his ancestral home and that was where he had to report for the Roman census. How then had he wound up in Nazareth? Large construction projects in Galilee were promising in terms of his livelihood. He was not planning to remain there permanently because when the Egyptian exile ended he intended to return with his family to Bethlehem. But then he was warned away from Bethlehem and detoured to Nazareth. The detour turned out to be propitious.

Not long after they arrived in Nazareth a new capital city for Galilee was built at Sepphoris, four miles away. Over the next three decades the construction of the city provided consistent work for Joseph and his carpenter's apprentice, Jesus. Furthermore, the city became a cosmopolitan gem in that part of the world, exposing Jesus to a richness of thoughts, ideas, and cultural benefits that would impact His remarkably sophisticated teaching ministry. It was a matter of timing, and God's timing is always the best timing.

The promise would be fulfilled, but not until the time was right — not until there was what the Bible calls "the fullness of time." The great historian Paul Maier has a book titled, *In the Fullness of Time*. Maier examines how in God's time and by God's power, circumstances came together at that precise point in human history to make the birth of Christ and the spread of the Church possible. During that brief span of years:

- For the first time in history, the whole Mediterranean world was united by a single language (Greek) — and that meant the message of Christ could spread more easily.
- For the first time in history there was a relatively secure peace across the known world. Historians call it *Pax Romana*, the

"Roman Peace"— and that meant missionaries of the faith could move about with freedom.

■ For the first time in history the nations of the world were linked by a network of roads and sea lanes, some of which are still in use today, and as a result, more people and nations could be exposed to the "good news of great joy" of which the angel sang.

■ For the first time in history, there was the devaluation of ancient pagan religions, and people were yearning for truth about the meaning of life — and that meant people's hearts and minds were fertile ground for the teachings of Jesus.

It was then, in the fullness of time, at the precise period when all those things were as they had to be and as they had never been before, it was then that the angel delivered the message to Joseph in a dream: "Take the child and go to the land of Israel. Be patient, but be hopeful. Ultimately God's promise of salvation will be fulfilled."

A thousand years before that happened to Joseph, a young Egyptian Pharaoh named Tutankhamun died. We know him as "King Tut." He was buried in the Valley of the Kings, together with some things it was believed he would need in the next life. Archaeologists found a basket of wheat seeds nestled among the jumble of priceless treasures in Tut's tomb. They took some of the seeds, planted and watered them, and waited. The warmth of the sun fell upon them, and they sprouted. Imagine. After lying dormant for 3,000 years — 30 centuries of dust and darkness — the seeds sprouted. The germ of life was in them all the while. Notice, though, that the seeds did not come to life on their own. It was not until an outside agency brought earth, water and sun that they could begin to flourish and capture a share of the immortality the mighty pharaohs had sought in vain.

The same is true for us. We do not have the power in and of ourselves to do what we ought to do. But God comes to us in Jesus Christ, the Son, and He fills us with hope that ultimately blossoms forth into salvation and eternal life. When God came down at Christmas and laid a baby on the world's doorstep, God gave us the way to let go of evil and claim good; the way to rid ourselves of fear, tension, guilt, and anxiety; the way to live triumphantly and victoriously even in the midst of the uncertainties of this world. God gave us salvation from our sins and the promise of eternal life. Christ is our hope even in the darkest of times. We see it in the experience of Joseph. When his life's journey seemed darkest, God gave Joseph the promise of hope — a hope postponed, but ultimately realized.

Temp Sparkman wrote a beautiful little book called, *To Live With Hope.* On its pages he recalls a trip home to Louisville, Kentucky. He and his family had moved to Kansas City, and this was the first time back in Louisville since their daughter, Laura Susannah, had died of leukemia. After visiting her grave in Louisville, Sparkman was moved to write: "It was October, but even autumn's painting, inspiring in its beauty, could not hold back the melancholy. Kneeling at Laura Susannah's grave, I rubbed my fingers across the etchings on the gravestone, perhaps unconsciously searching for some brailled cosmic words to heal the pain. I cried and waited in silence. Suddenly my ears were tuned to the October breeze. I tell you, in the hush, that wind carried Easter stirrings."[3]

Easter stirrings! Powerful phrase! That is the way God in Christ has revealed Himself in my life — faint stirrings of hope that have grown stronger with the passing of time. It did not happen suddenly; it happened across a number of years. But it was not until I was in college that I began to grasp what it all meant. I fell in love; I read a book; and I was gripped by the reality of Jesus Christ. Seem strange? In a way I suppose it is.

For three years in college I had tried to block out my Christian upbringing. Mind you, I did not descend into anything as dramatic as robbing a bank. It was more of a minor rebellion, but a rebellion just the same. For example, during my growing-up years, Sundays were held sacred: no work, no organized recreation, especially no Sunday afternoon movies. Wouldn't you know that on my first Sunday away at college I slept in, missed church, and then slouched off to a double feature. Silly and superficial as it may seem, it constituted a small step in the wrong direction.

During the next few years I continued to drift away from the Church and the Church's Lord. Faith slipped way down on the priority list of life. During my senior year I began to realize I had lost focus. My friends seemed to have such definite ideas about what they were going to do with their lives. I had no idea at all. I was floundering, and I knew it.

It was then that God brought into my life the beautiful blue-eyed girl who one day would be my wife. Trisha regarded Jesus Christ as being worth the commitment of her life. Occasionally we would talk about what faith in Christ meant. The subject was not foreign to me; I had grown up in the Church and was descended from a long line of ministers. But up to that point in my life, I was living their faith and not my own. It was my heritage, and I regarded it like an antique chair passed down through the generations – pleasant enough to behold, but you dare not place your full weight on it.

Then I read a book. I was taking a class in the philosophy of religion. Required reading for the course included Albert Schweitzer's *The Quest of the Historical Jesus*, a scholarly work that I read only because it was required. Surprisingly, the concluding words of the book hit me like a bolt out of the blue. The words remain carved into my memory:

> "He comes to us as One unknown, without a name, as of old, by the lake-side, He came to those men who knew Him not. He speaks to us the same word: 'Follow thou me!' and sets us to the tasks which He has to fulfill for our time. He commands. And to those who obey Him, whether they be wise or simple, He will reveal Himself in the toils, the conflicts, the sufferings which they shall pass through in His fellowship, and, as an ineffable mystery, they shall learn in their own experience Who He is."[4]

I did what Schweitzer suggested: I gave myself to as much of Jesus as I understood at that time. By so doing, I laid claim to the life-giving, life-changing, life-empowering relationship with Christ which is promised in Scripture. From that time until now Jesus Christ has exercised supreme control in my life. It has not been easy. It has not been all sweetness and light. I have let Him down more times than I care to remember, but He has never once forsaken me:

When I have called to Him...
   ...He has answered me .
When I have trusted Him...
   ...He has proven more than worthy of that trust.
When I have been weak...
   ...He has given me strength.
When I have been selfish...
   ...He has given me love.
When I have been sinful...
   ...He has given me pardon.
When I have reached the end of my rope...
   ...He has given me unconquerable hope.
When I have been lost...
   ...He has shown me the way home.

That is what this third dream was for Joseph: the stirrings of a hope deep within him. The angel said: "Take the child and head for the land of hope and promise. The victory will come, not immediately, but it will come. God will save you. That is God's solemn promise."

Here is the surpassing importance of this third dream to the Christmas story. It holds within it the promise of Easter. The same God who brought Jesus safely out of Bethlehem brought Jesus safely out of Egypt. And the same God who brought Jesus safely out of Egypt would bring Jesus safely out of Calvary. The message of Christmas is the message of Easter. The final victory of God — Hallelujah! — the final victory of

God over sin, evil and death is assured. It has not happened yet. It is a dream deferred, a victory postponed, a promise yet to be completely fulfilled. But that it will happen in God's good time and great mercy can never be doubted.

Remember the words of the carol:

No ear may hear His coming
But in this world of sin,
Where meek souls will receive Him,
Still the dear Christ enters in.

This is the great Good News of Christmas. Give Jesus leave to enter into your home and into your heart... and the Good News of Christmas will become Good News for your life.

⮰ DREAM FOUR ⮰

FULFILLMENT

"What kind of preacher do you have?" a man asked an acquaintance. "He is a lighter of lamps in a dark world," came the reply. Believe me, any preacher would be thrilled to hear such a review.

Joseph, of course, was not a preacher. So far as we know, he never spoke a word during that First Christmas. However, the more I have focused my mind and my heart upon this simple carpenter of Nazareth, the more convinced I have become that he, too, in his own way, was a lighter of lamps in a dark world. His actions provide illumination for our own journey through the darkness of this world.

Joseph's story reaches its crescendo in the fourth Christmas dream. Call it "Fulfillment." The message is crystal clear: Christmas is a gift from God wrapped in a marvelous mystery, containing a priceless treasure. Unwrap the gift and discover the treasure…

A Marvelous Mystery

God told Joseph in the dream to take the child to Nazareth, where the young Messiah would grow from childhood to adulthood. Nazareth was not much of a place. It is not mentioned a single time in the Old Testament. Most people believed that when the Messiah came He would come to one of David's cities, either David's birthplace in Bethlehem or his capital in Jerusalem. Certainly no one would have sought the Messiah in tiny Nazareth, a struggling hamlet no one had heard of, out in the middle of nowhere. Furthermore, the town was in Galilee, and the very name Galilee suggested a heavy Gentile popula-

41

tion. (*Galil ha goyim* - the Hebrew name for Galilee meaning "the region of the Gentiles.") Hard to imagine a more unlikely or more ignominious place to find the Messiah.

The lowliness of Jesus' childhood home prefigured His ultimate humiliation on the cross. If this Jesus were a king, He was a king like no other. Imagine Joseph's utter surprise when God told him: "Take the child to Nazareth." With a significance not to be missed, Joseph once more demonstrated his unwavering obedience to God. He took his little family to Nazareth.

Prophecy fulfilled. The prophets had predicted that the Messiah would be so ordinary and His arrival so inconspicuous that many people would miss Him. Nazareth was such a frightfully ordinary and inconspicuous place that it did not appear on maps of the day, and most people did not even acknowledge its existence.

The prophets also had foreseen that the Messiah would be scorned and ridiculed. Popular contempt for Nazareth was such that it was axiomatic that nothing good could come from the place. Even to be called a "Nazarene" was to suffer an insult, a slur, an epithet. The simple instruction of the angel to take the child to Nazareth is layered with complexities. It is the clear, unmistakable fulfillment of the Old Testament prophecies.

Joseph, knowledgeable in the Old Testament Scriptures, understood that. What Joseph would have had difficulty understanding is what many people still find difficult to understand: The child was God in human form.

Wait just a minute. The importance of this idea is so surpassing that we must make a detour, leaving the hills and woods of our journey with Joseph to take a long hard look at Joseph's son.

Peter the Great, Czar of all the Russias, periodically would lay aside his royal robes and don peasant garb. Thus able to enter the marketplace and mingle with the masses, he could listen to his subjects, feel their needs, sense their mood, know their longings. King *incognito*. The consequence of Joseph's fourth dream was that God, the King, was able to come down to this earth, wrapped in the ordinariness of a place called Nazareth, and grow to manhood among the simple, real people of His day. God incarnate. King *incognito*.

The American Dream holds that one of humble birth may rise from a log cabin to the White House. Jesus' story runs a reverse course. His is a not a story that begins in lowliness and rises to glory; instead it is a story that begins in glory and descends to lowliness. God laid aside the crown of heaven to become a carpenter's son. Jesus Christ became less than He was so that we might become more than we are. Joseph took the child to Nazareth.

Shocking, but true: A prominent minister stood before his congregation of several thousand people and declared, "Jesus is not the only begotten Son of God, but one of many. He is a man, not God."

That minister is a product of our age of broad-mindedness. Sadly, he is able to reach those who have come to regard Jesus as simply a notable figure who lived for a time, accomplished some significant things, and then passed away. These people congratulate one another for their insight that while Jesus' words may have some historical value and His style of living may offer useful guides for modern behavior, there is nothing divine with which to trouble themselves.

That school of thought is nothing less than a polite way of saying that Jesus is not adequate. It is a gentle – even sophisticated — way of removing Him from His central position as the world's best and only hope. Let's face it: It is a socially acceptable way of calling Jesus a well-intentioned liar, albeit with a gift for social engineering.

Ernest T. Campbell zeroes in on the truth: "God did not choose to save us by writing up in the sky, but by giving us a child, a cross, and an empty tomb." Not unlike the words of Simon Peter: "There is salvation in no one else, for there is no other name under heaven by which we must be saved."

Call it narrow, dogmatic, old-fashioned, unrealistic, intellectually inferior — call it whatever you wish. In an age when people seriously question the deity of Christ, I dare to stand with the Church through the ages and declare that Jesus, who grew up in the home of Mary and Joseph in Nazareth, is nothing less than God in human form, and there is salvation in no one else.

Ask me to explain it in a way that would satisfy those seekers who would reduce the Christ to nothing more than a gifted philosopher. I cannot. It is a mystery. But through this marvelous mystery, countless millions of people have found the secret of triumphant, victorious living. No one before or since has influenced the world as has Jesus of Nazareth.

■ He came into a world where the ruthless exercise of power turned the pages of history, but His was the way of love and peace.

■ He was never an academician, but His life challenges us to develop our mental capacity to love God all the more, and in His name thousands of schools and colleges have been founded.

■ He never wrote a line; no book bears His author's hand. But His teachings are universally known and quoted and have shaped the course of human history like no others.

■ He, though a carpenter by trade, never built any material objects of note, but we choose to honor Him through the matchless beauty of cathedrals, churches, and wayside chapels built to His glory.

■ He knew nothing of art, but His spirit ignites the creative spark in the human heart, and the art galleries of this world are graced with abundant expressions of who He was and who He is.

■ He never owned anything of value, yet when He died soldiers gambled for the only article in His estate, the seamless robe He wore. But everywhere His teachings are embraced the standard of living is lifted, and where His name is claimed no one can sit idly by when the needy go hungry and the lonely need a friend.

■ He spoke more of service than of rights and privileges, but where His message is heard and heeded, the value of every individual is exalted and the rights of all are protected, especially those who are weak and worn, forgotten and unborn.

■ He lived just thirty-three years before His life was cruelly ended, but He changed everything, even the way we date history. Surely we can agree with Paul that "His name is above every name."

It is the glorious mystery of Christmas that One who was wrapped in the common ordinary garb of Nazareth could be the Saviour of the world. But what a glorious, strengthening, empowering, life-giving, life-changing, death-defying, death-defeating mystery it is.

A Priceless Treasure

Now let's return to the main road of our journey. As the angel of the Lord in this fourth Christmas dream commanded, Joseph took God's own Son into his home in Nazareth and into his own heart. There the young Messiah would be exposed to the full range of human experience.

Have you ever wanted to cry out, "Nobody knows the trouble I've seen"? Remember the next words of the song: "Nobody knows but Jesus." Oh, yes, Jesus knew.

Jesus knew what it was to be a helpless child. He was born under circumstances which could leave any child marked with psychological trauma: rejection, privation, anxiety on the part of his parents, spirited away as an infant fugitive to evade political assassination.

Jesus knew what it was to be a teenager not understood by His parents. At age twelve He was engaged in stimulating discussion with the rabbis at the temple in Jerusalem. After a frantic search, His parents found Him where they least expected.

Hurt and frustrated, they demanded, "Son, why have you treated us so? We have been looking for you anxiously." Jesus replied with the raw edge of irritation in His voice, "Did you not know that I must be in my Father's house?"

Jesus knew what it was to lose a loved one to death. At some point in His early life, His earthly father, Joseph, died. Jesus assumed the heavy burden of the eldest son providing for His mother, His brothers and sisters. He knew what it was to rise at dawn and work until the sun's retreat. He knew what it was to saw and chisel, to file and plane, to shape wood and to cut stone. He knew what it was to be a businessman, to find the balance between supply and demand, to keep accurate financial records, to deal with customer complaints, to protect Himself against those who sought to take advantage of Him.

Jesus knew what it was to be a single, young adult. Surely He longed as any other person for the love of a spouse, the tenderness of a home, the joy of family. After all, having created those relationships, He knew their potential. Yet while the desire for love and marriage must have burned within Him, He knew what His life held in store. He could not knowingly ask a wife to share the road that lay ahead. All too soon she would be left a widow. Still He had deep need for companionship and for the presence of those who understood Him. He found that most often, I think, in the company of Peter, James and John, and in the home of Mary, Martha, and Lazarus.

Jesus knew hard times. He knew fatigue so great that He could sleep in a pitching boat in the middle of a storm. He knew such hunger for silence that some nights He just stayed out on the hills praying to the Heavenly Father and resting His weary bones. He experienced daily the loss of personal freedom, the pressure of crowds hanging on every word from His lips, the clutch of desperate people thrusting some loved one at Him for His healing touch. He knew what it was to watch His enemies marshal their forces to provoke the nasty confrontations that ultimately led to His death. He knew the temptation to remove Himself from submission to the will of God. Yet then He prayed the prayer of ultimate submission: "Father, not my will but thine be done."

We do not have a God who is beyond our human feelings, a God who cannot be touched by our trials and tribulations. Instead we have a God who in Jesus Christ became one of us and took up residence in the home of a carpenter named Joseph.

When Joseph took God's Son into his home in Nazareth the Gospel promise was fulfilled: "God so loved the world that He gave His one and only Son, that whoever believes in Him shall not perish but have eternal life."

Through all the years of my ministry I have never been able to preach from that text in John 3:16. I have alluded to it quite specifically in many sermons. I have included its message, I hope, in every sermon. But I have never actually preached from it because it is so far beyond my capacity to grasp. To think that God would come to this earth to live a life much like our own and to think that God would permit people not unlike you and me to take the life of His one and only Son! I cannot fully comprehend it. What I can say is that I am coming closer to comprehending it .

Just a few years ago our son, John David, was tragically killed at twenty-two years of age. In the aftermath of that devastating loss, I am just beginning to unlock the truth that where there is love between a father and his son, when you kill the son, you kill the father. That is what happened to God and His Son. God let it happen in order to identify completely with us in the human predicament and to give us the gift of a life that transcends our human limitations.

Furthermore, I do not think you can wrap your heart completely around John 3:16 until you understand what it meant for Jesus to live and grow up in the little town of Nazareth, with Joseph as His earthly father. Years later as Jesus engaged in His ministry of teaching He called God "Father." When Jesus wanted to say the best and highest thing He could say about God, He said, "He is like a loving and understanding father." Is it not reasonable to assume that what Jesus learned about being a father He learned from Joseph? Reach back into your mind and recall the clichés: "A twig grows in the direction it is bent." "The apple doesn't fall far from the tree." The words remind us of the relationship Jesus must have had with Joseph, and something about that relationship moved Jesus then to refer to God as "Father."

Read again some words from the song "Joseph's Lullaby." Joseph in his mind, is speaking to the infant Jesus:

> Tell me how to guide You,
> Tell me what to say.
> Tell me how to show You how
> To show the world the way.
> How to please the angels
> Watching from above
> When all I have to give You is love.

The song captures what I believe to be true. Joseph gave a lot to Jesus, but best of all was the love of a father.

How it must have been: *Jesus, as a little boy, would crowd His way into the workshop, and Joseph would always stop what he was doing to talk a spell about whatever the boy wanted to talk about, or to pick Him up and roll Him in the piles of soft sawdust until the bits of wood mingled with His dark, Jewish curls. Maybe it was this ready access to Joseph's shop and Joseph's attention which led Jesus later on to say, "Never prohibit a child from coming to Me."*

Did they go for long walks in the fields around Nazareth, stopping occasionally to pick flowers for Mary? Was it then that the seed was planted in Jesus' mind which later moved Him to say, "Consider the lilies of the field how they grow...even Solomon in all his glory was not arrayed like one of these."

As they walked together did Joseph tell the boy how they had escaped Herod's armies by taking that long, demanding, hazardous sojourn in Egypt? Was it then that Jesus began to tie into the concept of fatherhood the noble virtues of courage and bravery?

As they climbed higher into the nearby hills and came to places where flowing streams turned that desert-like place to lush green, was it then that Jesus began to imagine what it would be like to have streams of living water welling up within?

Reaching the summit where they could see caravan routes stretching out in all directions toward the horizon, was it then that Jesus began to mull in His mind the idea which later He would put into words, "Go into all the world and make disciples of all nations..."?

The lovely tenderness which Jesus saw Joseph give to Mary — was that what led the Master to exalt womankind to the highest level possible, a level never known before or since?

When Jesus spoke of talents — both money and ability — and the way we are to use them, were His thoughts shaped by the fact that He had seen Joseph develop his carpenter's skills to virtual perfection, and that He had watched Joseph pour everything of which he was capable into everything he did? And was it Jesus' appreciation for Joseph's work that led Jesus later to say so beautifully, "Take My yoke upon you, for My yoke is easy and My burden is light"?

When Jesus wanted us to know what God is like He said, "God is like a strong, brave, tender, loving, understanding Father." Where would Jesus have learned that if not from Joseph?

Here then is the greatest Christmas gift of all: God so loved that He gave His only Son. Joseph, the simple, unsophisticated carpenter of Nazareth, somehow understood that. Joseph brought Jesus up to seek the truth, but, of course, Jesus *is* the truth. Joseph showed Jesus all the love his heart could hold, but, of course, Jesus *is* love. Joseph gave Jesus a home, yes, but Jesus gave Joseph heaven. Joseph took God's Son into his home in Nazareth, thus providing Jesus with a normal, loving, family environment in which to grow. Joseph took God's Son into his heart, thus discovering a purpose for his own life within the greater purposes of God.

My prayer is that you will do the same.

Epilogue

Christmas 1981.

My family and I traveled to the Middle East. The trip was to be a spiritual pilgrimage for the five of us: Meg, Beth, John David, Trisha, and me. We were scheduled to be in Bethlehem on Christmas Eve. The experience turned out to be one of those events in life which burn themselves forever into the memory. It was a profoundly moving time for us, but it was also a time twisted with a terrible irony.

On Christmas Eve that year, Bethlehem was an armed camp. Only weeks before, Anwar Sadat had been assassinated in Egypt, and now the Palestine Liberation Organization was threatening a terrorist incident at Bethlehem. The whole region was in a state of unrest. As a result, heavily armed Israeli soldiers sealed off the little town of Bethlehem. Blockades were erected six miles away, on the outskirts of Jerusalem. Entrance into Bethlehem could be gained only by submitting to harsh and thorough security checks.

Expectantly, in retrospect naively, we approached the checkpoint at the Jerusalem blockade. Immediately our son, John David, and I were forcibly separated from Trisha and our daughters, Meg and Beth. At gunpoint, we were placed on separate buses and told that in due time we would be taken to Bethlehem. We were ordered to surrender our passports. There followed an extended time of inactivity on the part of the soldiers, coupled with rising anxiety on my part. Finally the buses, loaded primarily with soldiers, departed. At the outskirts of Bethlehem we were ordered off the bus. To our great relief we were reunited as a family, a reunion which proved to be short-lived.

Suddenly, once again, we were looking at the killing end of an Israeli machine gun. Short, crisp commands barked out by an Israeli officer indicated that we were to separate, male and

51

female, as before. We were then led to large, olive-drab military tents. We were completely searched, a process that involved some rough jostling by the soldiers whose tactics of intimidation were underscored by the ever-present, constantly prodding machine guns. To think that we had come to Bethlehem to celebrate the birth of the Prince of Peace!

At last we were escorted from the tents and released into Bethlehem's Manger Square. Before we could recover from the shocking experience at the hands of the soldiers, we were besieged by people trying to take advantage of the occasion to make as much money as they could, in any way that they could, by selling trinkets, souvenirs, and relics. As they clawed at us from every side, it seemed to me that their hunger for dollars had driven them mad. To think that we stood on the very ground where One whose peasant birth took place in the rude bareness of an animal feeding trough and whose adult life was marked by the fact that He had no place to lay His head!

Worse came to worst, and we found ourselves trapped in the midst of roaming bands of drunken, cursing young people, sadly most of them American. They seemed determined to submerge the loveliness of Christmas Eve under a sea of raucous and repulsive ugliness. To think that we had come to Bethlehem to pray to One who declared: "I have come to seek and to save the lost!"

It seemed to me then, and it seems to me still, to have been an act of God's grace, but we were led to slip away with a number of others from Manger Square to make our way out to the Shepherds' Fields. No more guns. No more hawkers. No more revelers. Just beauty...quiet beauty...with beautiful people. There were men, women and children from every part of the world — different colors, different languages, different nationalities, different dress, but all celebrating One Lord. There, on rocky, cave-pocked hillsides where so long ago shepherds heard the angels sing; there, as night slowly squeezed the last light out of the day and stars pierced the gathering darkness; there, together, our family was surrounded by the family of Christ. We sang our carols in five different languages. We read the Gospel stories. We prayed together. We wept together. We worshipped together. We felt as one in Christ and we felt at one with Christ. It was a feeling born there in Bethlehem, and it has never left me.

Seated on the rocky hillside that night, feet dangling down over the mouth of a small cave used then, and now, by Bethlehem shepherds to shield their flocks from stormy weather, I was captured — heart, mind, body, and soul — by the setting and the circumstance. My thoughts at that moment were riveted not on the shepherds or the angels or the Wise Men or even Mary, but on Joseph.

I tried to imagine what difficulties he faced that First Christmas. I, myself, had just tried to be protective of my family in the face of military force, and I experienced the ice-cold fear that grips a father's soul in that threatening circumstance. I, myself, had just attempted to maintain my religious equilibrium in the midst of a swirling secular chaos, and I experienced the sudden pangs of feeling inadequate to cope with something much bigger than I.

Joseph faced all of that in Bethlehem, and much, much more. Yet because he kept the channel clear both day and night to hear the directive of God, he was able not so much to triumph over the difficulties but to triumph in the midst of them. He so tuned the antennae of his soul to the guiding signals of God that he managed to bring the infant Jesus through all the hazards and hurts of that First Christmas.

Of course that did not spell the end of the trouble. Joseph saved Jesus' life that First Christmas only so that Jesus could later die for the salvation of the world. I could not help remembering a legend that tells of Jesus cultivating a garden as a young boy in Nazareth. In that garden He grew roses, and when they bloomed Jesus would plait them into garlands to adorn the hair. According to the legend, one day He asked some other children to come to the garden to play and to share the garlands. Instead, they tore the flowers from the stems and left the garden stripped and bare. Mockingly they cried, "How will you make your garlands now?" Jesus answered "You left the thorns."

O sing a song of Bethlehem
Of shepherds watching there;
And of the news that came to them
From angels in the air.

O sing a song of Calvary
Its glory and dismay;
Of Him who hung upon the tree
And took our sins away.

In Bethlehem that Christmas Eve I realized how the faithful response of Joseph to God's leading through the four dreams had issued forth into the salvation of the world. I resolved never again to shunt Joseph aside in the Christmas story.

It was at that point that my thoughts took a fascinating turn. I discovered that my own experience mingled with his. I tried to imagine what it would be like to be the designated father to the Lord of Glory.

The term "designated father" is my own. I understand it to mean "designated by God." I, too, am a "designated father." Because our three children are adopted, I have long been sensitive to the fact that there are two ways in which you can be a father. You can be a father *of* someone, and you can be a father *to* someone. To be a father of someone is simply a biological function. It has no great significance in and of itself. However to be a father to someone means to care for them, to love them, to teach them, to play with them, to provide for them, to be tolerant when intolerance would be easier, to be patient with them when impatience would be more natural. It is infinitely more difficult to be a father to someone than to be a father of someone.

I was not involved in the biological process that brought my children into this world. Yet God designated me to be father to them, and what joy that has brought me. I have not fulfilled the role perfectly, not by a long shot, but I have tried my best. Perhaps that is why I so trained my thoughts upon

Joseph, the designated father of Jesus. He had nothing to do with the miraculous biological process that resulted in the birth of Jesus, but he was a father to Jesus, giving Jesus both his home and his heart.

We dare not forget that God had all the men in this world from whom to pick when He selected a father for Jesus. God picked Joseph. What an incredible man the carpenter of Nazareth must have been!

The forgotten man of Christmas?

No more...

Endnotes

1.   Dietrich Bonhoeffer, *Life Together* (New York: Harper and Row, 1954), 23.

2.   David A. Redding, *Amazed by Grace* (Old Tappan, New Jersey: Fleming H. Revell Co., 1986), 74.

3.   Temp Sparkman, *To Live with Hope* (Valley Forge: Judson Press, 1985), 105-106.

4.   Albert Schweitzer, *The Quest of the Historical Jesus* (London: A & C Black,1926), 401.

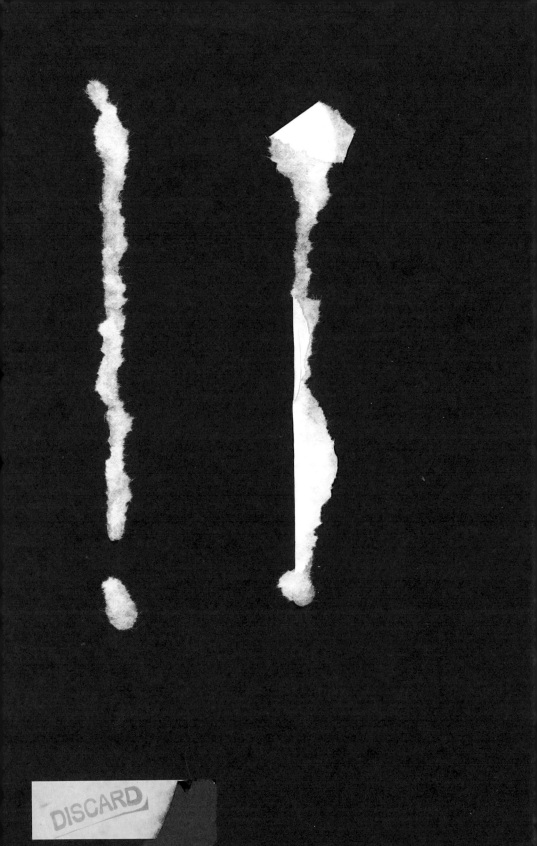